The Horse's Name Was Physics

The Horse's Name Was Physics

Poems by George Drew

Turning Point

© 2006 by George Drew

Published by Turning Point
P.O. Box 541106
Cincinnati, OH 45254-1106

Typeset in Baskerville by WordTech Communications LLC,
Cincinnati, OH

ISBN: 1933456205
LCCN: 2006901781

Poetry Editor: Kevin Walzer
Business Editor: Lori Jareo

Visit us on the web at www.turningpointbooks.com

Acknowledgments

Grateful thanks to the editors of the following publications for poems that originally appeared in them:

The Journal of Kentucky Studies: "FDR & Me," "The Genius to be Astonished," "The Journey of Death"

The Quarterly: "The Day the Sand Began to Hop," "Ahimsa" (each under the title, "Poem")

The Snail's Pace Review: "Back From the Vanishing Point"

Acknowledgment is also due to Richard Rhodes and his wonderful book, *The Making of the Atomic Bomb* (Simon and Schuster, 1986); much of the material in my poems was suggested by what I read. Thanks, too, to Kevin Gavitt, who knows his physics and helped me to know what little I can call mine. Finally, and most especially, thanks to Christopher Bursk, David Dooley, Bruce Gregory, Allen Hoey, Gray Jacobik, Meg Kearney, Harry Staley, and Baron Wormser, whose unstinting care and always cogent criticism helped to give this book its final shape.

For

>*John Murray,*
>
>>*Marty Lewis,*
>>
>>>*Warren Joscelyn*

If I don't kill that rat he'll die.

—Clov

Contents

The Characters 11

The Horse's Name Was Physics 17
Wild Beasts in the Ruined Cornfields 18
Clara's Calling 20
The Icehouse 22
The Night That Nature Spoke 24
The Dream of Doves..25
The Birds of Passage and the Goats..27
All Things Being Equal 29
The Different Meanings of the Word I 31
Wooden Tables and a Piece of Paraffin 33
The Genius to be Astonished..35
The Day the Sand Began to Hop 37
Back From the Vanishing Point..38
The Other I Inside the I 39
Queer Animals and Tomato Plants 41
FDR & Me..43
Supping with the Devil..44
The Day the Moon Lost All Its Shine 46
Ahimsa...47
A First Good Look 48
Beyond the Fields of Bright Aster 52
The Journey of Death 54
When Chloroform No Longer Works.....................................57

Notes 59

The Characters

The events referred to occur in the period from World War I to the first atomic explosion in July, 1945. In a few of the poems the speakers are fictive and anonymous; the rest are listed in the order in which they appear, together with the people about whom they are speaking. The date heading each poem refers to either the events depicted or the date on which the narrator is speaking, the context making clear which it is.

ERNEST RUTHERFORD (1871-1937): Discovered the nucleus. Director of the Cavendish Laboratory in Manchester, England. Both he and Bohr admired the young English physicist, HARRY MOSELEY (1887-1915). Moseley was killed at Gallipoli.

CLARA HABER (1871-1915): The first woman to receive a doctorate in chemistry from the University of Breslau, she was the wife of FRITZ HABER (1868-1934), the great chemist who led the development of poison gases for the Kaiser, overseeing their first use on the battlefield at Ypres. Clara Haber committed suicide.

WERNER HEISENBERG (1901-1967): Established the Uncertainty Principle—the idea that you can't measure a particle without affecting it. All you can do is, statistically, posit probabilities of future particle behavior—hence the universe is random.

LEO SZILARD (1898-1964): The existentialist of the atom, stressing moral responsibility. He saw early on the profound ethical dilemmas posed by nuclear physics—especially as applied to weaponry. Reminding the community of physicists of this was his particular gift.

ALBERT EINSTEIN (1879-1955): The second Newton. Other than the genius he was, the fascinating thing about him was the ultimate dilemma of his life: his visceral inability to accept the implications of the very universe he'd helped to reveal. The quantum was his Waterloo.

ROBERT OPPENHEIMER (1904-1967): The dark angel of Los Alamos. He was the director of the Manhattan Project—the development of the first atomic bomb. He was a genius, but a genius divided. He drove, but was driven.

NIELS BOHR (1885-1962): One of the two great physicists of the century. He established the experimentally accurate model of the atom, at its center the release of energy due to the "hopping" of electrons from one "shell" to another. Later came his theory of "complementarity," which sought to reconcile dualities—for instance, wave and particle. Above all others, Bohr foresaw the philosophical implications of the quantum.

G.C. TRABACCHI (dates unknown): Was the chief physicist for Rome's Sanità Pubblica, its health department. He kept ENRICO FERMI (1901-1954) and his group supplied, and in general lent assistance as he could. Fermi developed the theory of beta decay, and established the "weak force," one of the four fundamental forces of the universe.

LISE MEITNER (1878-1968): The aunt of OTTO FRISCH (1904-1979). She and Frisch worked out the electron volts that are released when the uranium atom splits, thus verifying the theory of OTTO HAHN (1879-1968). Hahn, in 1938, first split the atom of uranium, the breakthrough that would lead to the atomic bomb.

LÈON ROSENFELD (1904-1974): Belgian physicist who was something of an acolyte to Niels Bohr, traveling with him and working with him on electron theory.

MARK OLIPHANT (1901-2000): An Australian physicist. As the head of the physics department at the University of Birmingham, he brought Otto Frisch to England, getting him a job as lecturer. Later, at Los Alamos, Frisch would work on what was called the Dragon Experiment—critical masses necessary for a chain reaction in the Bomb.

EDWARD TELLER (1908-2003): One of the two "fathers" of the hydrogen bomb, who pushed for its development, and ultimately found himself at the center of the storm over the development of nuclear weaponry. Ironically, in the beginning he'd had real reservations about the whole idea of making an atomic bomb.

AAGE BOHR (1922-): The youngest son of Niels Bohr and himself a Nobel Prize recipient.

EMILIO SEGRÈ (1905-1989): One of the Fermi group in Rome. He has been described as bright and articulate. Later, in fact, he went on to win a Nobel Prize—and write a history of modern physics. Worked on the Bomb at Los Alamos.

JAMES CHADWICK (1891-1974): Discovered the neutron in 1932, thus opening the nucleus to detailed study. Though one of the major milestones in nuclear physics, Chadwick made what C. P. Snow said was "one of the shortest accounts ever made about a major discovery," then said he wanted to be chloroformed and put to bed for a couple of weeks. Later, when he realized the Bomb was inevitable, sleeping pills became a daily regimen.

The Horse's Name Was Physics

The Horse's Name Was Physics

The horse's name was Physics,
and they rode it well.
The only difference was this:
some chose to flog the horse,
some flogged themselves.

Wild Beasts in the Ruined Cornfields

Manchester
September 1915

Dear Bohr,
             It's happened. Moseley's dead at Gallipoli.
I have it from good sources he died bravely, even,
as much as such a thing is possible in the very bowels
of Hell, contented, having willed his meagre assets,
all of them, to Science. You recall, don't you,
how Spartan he was in his days with me,
living on cheese and fruit? And he was just
as Spartan in his friendliness. God,
how he rankled! So aloof. So stuffy, upper-class.
And even here in Manchester he disliked foreigners,
their smell. The Hindu. Burmese. Jap. Vile Indians.
But in a war in which the smell of new-mown hay
and blossoming lilac sends the soldiers running
for their lives, that he died at the hands
of foreigners should not surprise. Awful, yes.
But mathematical, exact—there in the heat
of those ruined cornfields, with the knives
and stones leaping from human hands;
the bodies of the Turks two-deep, four-deep,
six-deep. Of course we weep—especially you,
whose nay-sayers he nailed to the cross
of their own doubt, the spectral lines he spent
a beastly summer labouring to count his nails.
But he liked action, able, as you know, to work
for fifteen hours at a stretch, and after weeks
on that horrible beach with nothing but centipedes
and flies, chlorodyne for the bowels, and jam
from home for the soul, even death must have lost
its sting. So let us weep, for he is gone.
But, as he knew, the destination never was

in doubt—the universe, the ultimate nucleus,
ad infinitum. And him the neutron lodging deep.
As are we all, dear Bohr. As are we all.
                              Yours,
                                    Rutherford

Clara's Calling

Berlin
Autumn 1915

My Dearest Fritz,
             What is it Rutherford says about atoms?
Like flies in a cathedral? Flies in a morgue, I'd say.
A morgue so full of corpses there's no room for more.
I see them clearly: bodies red and cracked,
eyes swollen shut, hands clutching at throats,
mouths open in a soundless scream, the tongues
twisted in agony and hanging out like snakes. This,
Herr Haber, is your gift to Germany, all these
young soldiers who did not have time to learn
the danger in the smell of new-mown hay
and in the lilac bushes blossoming in the Belgian
countryside; who were the first victims
of your handiwork—those gases multiplying, changing
shape, diversifying like Darwin's finches, hovering
in the deadly fields of Belgium, France…. My God!
Why can't I make you see? Yes, you! The one
with whom, since childhood, I was going to bring
about a new world founded on a science serving love,
the kind of love I've given to you since we first met
on a dance floor. Do you remember? Dance we did,
bodies close, souls, minds. Oh Fritz, tell me,
what happened to the dance? I've given you a child,
I gave you me, a home, a life, a love—and all
for what? This supervision of a death. That awful gas.
My own husband, the Judas of his craft—our craft,
the chemistry that was to fashion our new world.
And what, the silver pieces clinking in your pocket,
do you say?—*two bodies now will save four later.*
Poor, poor Fritz. You see nothing but what you see.
Two bodies now? My husband, that's the mathematics

of the mad. This haunts me, haunts me even in my sleep,
what little I can manage; haunts me like a cloud,
a fog, of your concoctions seeping through my dreams,
the way your mustard gas does clothing, flesh,
the organs, cells.... I've argued, fought, demanded,
even begged that you recall the world we knew would,
by our work, one day be grander by a factor far
past reckoning. But you've gone now, storming out
into the night, asserting that your country owns you
during war, that the world is nothing. Nothing,
dearest, is all I've left to give. It's my calling,
and I give it now to you, just as you've given it
to all those fine young men. Goodbye, my husband.

Love,

Clara

The Icehouse

Camp Koenig
Summer 1918

It was spooky—those blocks of ice stacked
on every side, like dice no one could throw,
that awful yellow light the single bulb
gave off, our faces jaundiced in its glare,
and every breath a vicious little ghost
we'd called back from the other side
especially for him. Don't get me wrong,
I'm not so proud of what we did
that night in the camp's icehouse. Hell,
he couldn't help the way he looked: so thin
and dark and baby-faced. He *was* a Jew.
That wasn't the problem. And anyway,
we didn't say too much of anything
to him all summer long, except for how
we weren't so sure he was a boy. And that
was true—until we stripped him down
that night. The problem was his folks,
just plain bad luck for him, I guess.
We weren't exactly what you'd call
the best of friends, he and I, but we
shared bunks—him on the bottom, naturally.
And so we talked. He told me once
the problem was, for all of his 14 years
they wouldn't let him meet the world
and its hard facts head-on, and how
he couldn't be the bastard that the world
required. They quarantined him like a germ.
And then, whenever he'd break free,
they'd come on the run at the least
sign of trouble. Next he knew,
he'd have all hell to pay, the way
he did that night in the icehouse.
What he'd done is written them and said

he'd learned some of the harder things
about life from us. So here they came,
running to the director of the camp,
who put his size-ten foot down
on our dirty jokes, and us. Well,
that was that. "Oppenheimer," we said,
"you're dead." He ended up that night
buck-naked in the icehouse, no way to run,
with twelve angry boys circling him.
We wanted him to beg, or at least cry,
for mercy. I'll never forget how he
just stood there, lips gone blue
from the cold, and stared straight back
at us, his eyes as bright and hard
as all the rocks he'd gathered on the hikes
he liked to take—alone of course.
It drove us nuts, the way he always said
"no thanks" to raising hell with us,
but now *his* were in our hands. God knows,
we hadn't meant him any pain. But he laughed,
he actually laughed! He stood there,
naked as the day his mother gave him life,
and laughed—at us! That did it. Fists
came at his body, pounding hard and fast,
his stomach, ribs, his head, until he sank
to the floor sweating fiercely, cold or not.
And then, as God's my witness, what we did
was paint his ass and privates green,
gathered up his clothes, and left him there,
bloodied and dripping paint. But you know,
he never said a word, and worst of all,
he didn't fight. That really got to us,
I guess, his taking our abuse, and all
the time that look in his eyes that said
oh it's all right, I understand....
I'm not proud, but I'm not ashamed of it.
He brought it on himself. And he was lucky.
In one short night he learned to be a bastard.

The Night That Nature Spoke

Copenhagen
Winter 1927

It was March, but my quick stride excited me
the way heat will an atom, and the night
became as balmy as a night in early spring
as I walked past the great beech trees
behind Bohr's institute onto the football field.
Above me even the stars, fixed little chunks
stuck to the heavens, argued Bohr's conviction
that all matter was granular. Then,
across the sky due north I saw one streak,
a wave of brilliance summarizing everything.
Which would it be? Particle or wave?
Who was correct? Bohr or Schrödinger?
It was a cosmic football match, the ball
whizzing back and forth, two perfect teams,
no winners and no losers. It was the kind
of beauty that murders little minds.
Was I going mad? In that moment I was
inside the atom, neutrons coming at me hard
and fast, battering me into eternal dark.
I was Schrödinger's cat, there in the box
if someone lifted the lid, and not there
if the lid stayed shut. And it was then,
in the emptiness of that most total night,
that darkness lifted like a heavy fog.
Suddenly nature spoke to me. And I saw
there was another beauty, one that blurred
the divine right of our senses, particles
the democrats *par excellence* of everything.
And certain of all uncertainty I went in
and slept for the first time in months.

The Dream of Doves

London
12 September 1933

In those days, when I still had my health,
I was the gypsy of the physics set,
living from suitcases in rented rooms
and dining alone in badly-lit cafes
in Budapest, Berlin, Vienna, Rome—
wherever I happened to be. I was adept
at being a step ahead of events;
so adept I even made it out of Berlin
and into Austria, beating the Nazis
by a day, the empty train I'd taken
one day stuffed with Jews the next
and stopped at the border by the SS.
From Austria I made my way to London,
where I saw the future on a cold,
gray morning on Southampton Row
as the streetlight I was waiting on
turned green—a future only a mind
as random as the grainy particles
of matter could have broken through to
in a chain reaction of the gray stuff
in my head, ideas bombarding ideas,
each doubling like the neutrons I knew,
in the truth of that moment, would.
Was I mad? Would the world come to say
of me, "Oh, that was just Szilard—
one of those crazy physicists who
thought he could save the world"?
Maybe, but I was thirty-five and naïve
enough to believe in my own vision.
Climbing an Everest wasn't important;
having the idea that you could—
this was everything. In that instant,

on a wet day, as I crossed a street
in Russell Square pooled by green light,
I dreamed of doves, of a peace that would
outlast Herr Hitler's thousand years,
and in my dreaming couldn't see
the vultures I was letting loose.
Save the world indeed! Right then,
before I'd even reached the other curb,
the future put a stop to doves,
the world evaporating to the shadow
of a child smeared on a stone wall,
the stuff of life, that brilliant star,
exploding into tyranny. The light went red.

The Birds of Passage and the Goats

Roughton Heath,
England
25 September 1933

My Dearest Elsa,
                I've arrived safely. Is it only three months
since my third and final rendezvous with Flexner there
in our own home? The home I told you we'd not see again?
You disagreed, I know. "Caputh, and Germany, will still be
here," you said. "You'll see." Indeed, my dove, I *have* seen.
We talked all day, Flexner and I. The deal was struck.
"Flexner," I said, "Ich bin Feuer und Flamme dafür."
I am fire and flame for it—America. We shook hands.
Princeton would be our new Caputh. First, though,
at your insistence, here—the cold North Sea and Roughton Heath,
the English weather, its relentless damp and mist, the clouds
charging in from a sea as strangely gray as the man
who'd bundled me off to this bleak place on the coast.
Commander Locker-Lampson was his name—a man
who'd once been asked by the Czar himself to kill Rasputin!
Ich bin Feuer und Flamme dafür? How these words haunt me,
Elsa, as I walk out onto the moors, alone except for the wind,
and the goats. I talk to the wind, but the wind does not talk
back. So now I talk to the goats, and the goats go
on chewing. Frisch, Pauli, Born and Bohr, Wigner
and Teller, Bethe and Szilard. So many birds
of passage on the way to a distant land. I walk
among the goats, head bent to the wind, and talk of them.
Could things be worse? Could *anything* be worse? And then,
dear Elsa, I heard—just this morning. Ehrenfest.
Poor Ehrenfest, the noblest of us all, has tried, and failed,
to kill his youngest son, leaving him blind—and fatherless.
Ehrenfest, my friend, has killed himself. And so I walk,
and tell the goats about a mass heavier even than
my sadness, mass imploding like poor Ehrenfest's heart
into dead worlds. *Ich bin Feuer und Flamme dafür?* Yes,

but the question is, will it be freed by us, or we by it?
The goats nod back, but they don't know. My dear,
Belgium is worlds from here, and worlds are lonely—like
these moors. Come safely, but come with haste.
Your Own,
Albert

All Things Being Equal

Berkeley
Winter 1934

Dear Einstein:

In Spanish nothing's *nada*, and in Latin *nihil*.
I don't know what it is in Danish, but I know
Bohr does. He's lost a child. And now,
if you'd no chance before, you've even less.

You'll not convince him God's no gambler.
Never. Not now. For him, God's nothing
but the dice. And we're the ones who lose.
God's handiwork has made damned sure of that.

For him, the quantum is, arguments aside,
the one true Jacob wrestling with an angel
that's as possible as not. The Öresund
was cold, and that was everything.

It wasn't just the sudden squall, nor his
son's having fallen overboard. He was,
in fact, a more than capable sailor,
like his father, and a good swimmer, too.

It was the cold—a cold as harsh, he said,
as the ice so necessary to the dream he'd had
for weeks: there was a lake in winter, ice,
him on his stomach at the edge of a black hole,

and a useless limb beside him on the ice.
The Öresund was cold, and his beloved boy
had disappeared as quickly as the dream
after it was no longer just a dream.

And as for particles and waves, can you
think of anything more granular than his
sad heart? For hours he'd circled like
a neutron looking for a way to penetrate

until there was no light. Is the wave more
truthful than the particle? The particle
more than the wave? Is what is there
more truthful when we look or when we don't?

$E=MC^2$ indeed! This has, then, much to do
with nothing. If, as twilight settled over
him like a sudden agitation of the shells
from which the bold electrons leap,

he'd counted every atom, *ad infinitum*,
then counted backward, would it matter?
At either end of the progression there
is nothing. And this nothingness divides

and subdivides into an isotope of the unknown.
But nothing can be everything if nothing's
all you have. So nothing's everything.
Sometimes. It's also true that everything

is nothing. Nothing, then, equals everything,
and everything nothing.... Oh, damn it,
Albert, the Öresund was really cold, but all
things being equal, I know he will endure.
                              Yours,
                                    Oppenheimer

The Different Meanings of the Word I

Copenhagen
Winter 1934

Dear Einstein:

You ask how I am. I imagine, if I said
God doesn't play with dice but likes
to see them roll, you'd say, "Poor Bohr,
he imagines God plays with His own laws."

Once, when I was a boy, my father said,
during an evening stroll, that trees
were their constituent parts: the roots,
the trunks, the branches, limbs and leaves.
"No, no, " I said, "the whole thing is a tree."

How right I was, and yet how wrong.
Consider me: just shy of fifty years ago
on one small planet mass evolved from energy.
And I was me. Or me was I. Or I *and* me.

Now, walking deep into a month when we
are deep in snow and somehow something has
triggered the cold's most finite trap,
I wonder if I sees: what's I, what's me,
and, finally, what's not. Is not-I and not-me.

I wonder if me thinks of where I's going.

I say it's not a question of importance,
only that you know your unimportance
and become important in the knowing—
mass, that is, to energy and back again,
eternal transmutation. Call it God.

Kierkegaard, poor tortured Kierkegaard,
said we must make a choice: the Or
or Either, not the Neither or the Nor.
In other words, Albert, the dice do roll.
                              As Ever,
                                      Bohr

Wooden Tables and a Piece of Paraffin

Rome
March/June 1934

Fermi? You want to know what I know about Fermi?
What I know is what the men around him, back
then, evidently didn't: that he was, in fact,
the Michelangelo of atoms, preferring the chisels
of the laboratory to the physicist-philosophers
he couldn't understand—like Heisenberg.
Those young men called him Pope, the atom's emissary
here on earth. And I could see their point. He *was*
infallible in matters of the quantum. Even our building
must have seemed a Vatican, set as it was on a green hill
within a park in central Rome, the garden laced
with palm trees and bamboo, the gravel path a sparkling white
in the hot sun. And it was silent, as the Sistine must
have been for Michelangelo when he was locked in
painting it. Birds were the only things that broke
the peace, and then only at dusk when sparrows took
to the trees. So Pope it was. And who was I,
Trabacchi, to argue? I too a physicist, yes,
but for Public Sanitation, and in my spare time
a scholar of the arts. Providence. That's what
he and his young men called me back then. Divine Provider,
one who kept the tools and the supplies they needed
coming. Better, though, they'd called me Urbino—
servant to the end. For, truly, I thought he was more
a Michelangelo—a Master releasing, not the image,
but the energy of stone, the energy of stars, of suns.
Of everything! He was a sculptor, not of stone,
of marble, but of what stone was, the marbleness
of marble, that which is the grace of marble made
alive to touch. Like Michelangelo, by capturing he set
free—the fire, the blinding flames of all we see,
and what we don't. Could you have seen him racing
down a long hallway, his lab coat flying, you

too would have thought him more than merely Pope,
the earthly diplomat for God. And wasn't he
like Michelangelo? You should have seen the way
he took on Nature: measuring the height of trees,
the distance to a range of mountains, and the speed
of birds in flight. Like Michelangelo his stone,
he measured neutrons, slowing them with wooden tables
and a piece of paraffin. Tables and a wax! On one
amazing day he went away to lunch, pondered
the mysteries of paraffin and wood, and then
returned and painted the ceiling of the universe:
it was, he said, the nuclei of hydrogen. Now
do you see? Pope wasn't right. Terribilità—*that*
was him, the man I knew back then, and who knew me.
The nuclei of hydrogen. Was there more to say? Maybe,
but he didn't, and wouldn't now. Painting the ceiling
was enough. He left the altar wall to someone else.

The Genius to be Astonished

Bologna
20 October 1937

Whether he was trimming a tree
or pruning the mysteries of the atom,

you could see it in his eyes,
so twinkling and blue,

and in his cheeks,
so red when he blushed

they were like the berries
of the virgin miro trees

from which he'd shot pigeons
on his New Zealand farm

when he was a boy
and free of being wrong.

Then came the atom,
and what was that but one

of those potatoes
he'd sworn to never dig again?

A void within a void,
a no-potato wrapped by a no-skin.

The day arrived,
the alpha particles scattering,

coming back at him
as if the bullets were returning

to the gun,
the pigeons he'd shot

springing back into the miro trees,
time turning on itself.

Clearly this was no potato
rotting in the dim and dank air

of the basement he preferred
to root out error in.

Clearly it had a heart,
and so did he,

only that thing around
his small intestine

strangling life until it snapped.
And what are we to do

but what he did that day,
his big belly oscillating

like excited atoms.
Smile.

The Day the Sand Began to Hop

Stockholm
3 January 1939

Dear Hahn,
          Please rest assured: your fantasy's no fantasy.
You've split uranium. Frisch, as you know, was in Kungälv
with me. Like you, we thought the way to fission was
a muddle. Then we went for a walk to work it out—
or rather, *I* went for a walk. Frisch skied. A lovely day—
which must have done the trick. We stopped, I drew
a picture. "Couldn't this be it?" It, of course, was
Bohr's model of the atom—his so-called "liquid-drop."
When it is hit by a neutron it oscillates. A waist
is formed, and then the waist gives way. You know
the math: two nuclei where there was one. The rest
is pure Einstein—the weight of the two nuclei less
than the original. Now factor that through Albert's $E=MC^2$
and you come out with what it takes to pull the nuclei
apart: 200 million electron volts. And there you have it—
all that energy. It's beautiful. Frisch says he feels
as though he's caught an elephant by the tail. Imagine it:
the energy from every nucleus would make a grain
of sand begin to hop. An elephant indeed. Or would
a dragon be more apropos? Congratulations, Otto.
                                                  Meitner

Back From the Vanishing Point

New York
25 January 1939

TO: LEWIS STRAUSS
    c/o KUHN, LOEB ASSOCIATES

FOR TWO YEARS NOW MY DREAM HAD VANISHED STOP I'D GIVEN UP STOP BUT LIKE THE ELECTRON JUMPING BACKWARD FROM ITS OUTER SHELL THE DREAM IS MINE AGAIN STOP URANIUM HAS GIVEN WAY STOP YOU OF COURSE KNOW WHAT THIS MEANS STOP I LEARNED OF IT FROM WIGNER SICK IN PRINCETON STOP WHO GOT IT VIA THE INFIRMARY STOP WHICH GOT IT IN TURN FROM WHEELER ET AL IN NEW YORK STOP WHO LEARNED OF IT FROM ROSENFELD STOP WHO GOT IT FROM BOHR EN ROUTE ON THE ATLANTIC TO NEW YORK STOP WHO LEARNED OF IT FROM FRISCH IN COPENHAGEN STOP WHO GOT IT IN KUNGÄLV FROM HIS AUNT MEITNER STOP WHO HAD IT STRAIGHT FROM HAHN IN DAHLEM STOP WHO SAYS A CHAINREACTION ISN'T POSSIBLE?

SZILARD

The Other I Inside the I

Washington
29 April 1939

Placzek—it was all his fault, contesting Bohr's liquid-drop
model of the atom so vociferously over bacon and eggs that
morning. Princeton was beautiful in winter—from the inside.
But the next thing I knew, we were off, Bohr and I,

tramping through snow and cold across campus and to work.
And what work! In Einstein's office it occurred. With all
respect to Peirels' window-and-balls analogy for nuclei
bombardment by neutrons, he said, we've been throwing all

our balls at the same window. There were really two,
and only slow and well-aimed balls would enter them.
He had it all, he said, and broke piece after piece
of chalk in sharing it with me. U235, he said, that

was the truth of it, and drew three graphs on the board.
How it amazed me! Those three sets of curving lines inside
three perfect L's, and in an instant one improbability
turned real. It's U235, he said, that's fissionable, not

U238. He looked at me, fired up his pipe, and smiled.
Let's go, he said, and led me back the way we'd come,
this time a puckish smile curling around the stem
of his big pipe, and the snowballs a group of boys

were throwing whizzing through the air. We were halfway
across the campus when suddenly he stopped. This time,
he said, the I would not escape—the other I, the one
inside the I the world says is him. The question,

Rosenfeld, he said, is what would happen if we separate
the I from the I inside? Identity is what he seemed
to be talking about, but I knew what he really meant—
the U235. What if we isolated it from all the U238?

From his pipe the smoke, a thin gray tower, rose
into the winter air, hovered a moment, and then dispersed.

Queer Animals and Tomato Plants

Birmingham
March 1940

           When he first arrived here in Birmingham,
"Mr. Oliphant," Frisch said to me, with a look of pure
longing in his eyes, "In Hamburg, just a year ago,
life was never better." I could see his point. By day
his lab, and thought by night. He'd sit for hours
with a sheet of paper and a reading lamp,
the numbers crowding his mind as real to him
as all the animals early men drew on the walls
of their deep caves. He'd work, he said, until he'd see
queer animals against the background of his room.
He never knew exactly what they were, but he'd see
enough to frighten him into bed by one o'clock,
and into sleep, which always made them go away.
Imaginary creatures in a time so wonderful it seemed
imaginary, too.
           And then, like any tourist, off he came
by train and boat to England, here to where he found,
with Peirels, real animals that breathed real fire.
Fast neutrons were the prize inhabitants. The bomb
was possible. It staggered them, the thought of all
those dragons, but it could be done, and with far
less uranium than anyone had thought: only a pound
or two. It was inevitable. The animals were massing
at the gate. Someone, and all too soon, in the dead
of a dark night, would slip the bolt, and out
the animals would come, the fire of their most terrible
breath consuming all in their path. Something was bound
to happen, and soon.
           This isn't Hamburg, but Frisch
says the excitement of the work makes him forget,

and sometimes, turning to Peirels, he'll call him Stern.
And then, of course, he'll remember Otto Stern is still
in Germany, that *this* is Birmingham and *that* is Peirels,
and his face will go beet-red. Remarkably red!
The major difference, though, is fear. One afternoon,
the weather being nice, the window in the lab
was open. As they worked to train the animals,
a face appeared in the window. *Hitler!* Frisch yelled.
The gate! The gate! He's come to open the gate!
But no, it was tomatoes. The man Frisch thought
was Hitler had planted them beneath the window
and had come to see if they were doing well. Frisch laughed.
Peirels laughed. But the animals were excited, and they
could feel the heat. It's clear it won't be long
before the bolt will be released.
                                              It had better be by us.

FDR & Me

Washington
May 1940

Szilard,

>You men must rally round the atom's might,
>he said that day, his voice bombarding us.
>You must not hesitate in this good fight.
>
>As soon as he began I saw the light,
>each sentence wrapping me in its embrace.
>I, too, must rally round the atom's might.
>
>And all of you, he said, must put to flight
>your doubts. The world is as it always was.
>You must not hesitate in this good fight.
>
>He speaks to me, I thought. And he is right.
>It's not our fault. The world is mad, not us.
>I, too, must rally round the atom's might.
>
>It's up to you, he said, to keep the light
>of freedom glowing in the dark. God knows,
>you must not hesitate in this good fight.
>
>Never, I swore. I, too, have seen the light
>of freedom snuffed. And lived to keep these vows.
>I, too, will rally round the atom's might.
>And will not hesitate in this good fight.

Teller

Supping with the Devil

Leipzig
November 1941

Here's how it went with Bohr. "Heisenberg,"
he said, "had I come there to Germany
we would have sat on a park bench
and talked for a long while of elements,
of electrons jumping like mad acrobats."
But he hadn't. I went there,
to Denmark. That, in his eyes, made me
suspect. It hadn't always been that way.
Once, hiking through the chaos of rocks
up one last mile to a wind-stricken peak,
I was stunned by the tiny flowers that
huddled in the shadows of the overhangs
of rocks. "Such lovely, delicate things
to be so adamant," I said, and thought:
forget-me-nots. But they weren't.
And so I named them *Bohr*. Like him,
although they wrap themselves in dark,
they light the mind, their flowers so
damned showy in the alpine wind.
Then, when I met him there,
in Copenhagen, "Heisenberg," he said,
"we ought to go for a long walk,"
and I that I'd come for his advice.
Though we talked, it soon was clear
he thought I'd come to find out what
he knew. I said that wasn't so,
and gave him, at some risk, a sketch
of the reactor I'd been working on.
He said he understood that any man
must serve his country during war,
I that he'd misconstrued. He thought
I had been supping with the devil with
a spoon that was too short. I said

not so, and he that he would never be
the guest. I said I hadn't asked him to.
He said goodbye. That's how it went.

The Day the Moon Lost All Its Shine

Chicago
2 December 1942

Nightmares are always black. And it was black
from the beginning: graphite dust on lab coats,
goggles, hands and faces—everything. Only teeth
shone white in all that black. And they were chattering.
It was so cold the guards were wearing raccoon coats.
Cold weather for the hottest day in history.
How's that for paradox?—as pure as the uranium
in our huge pile. It was freezing, and it also was
the second day of petrol rationing. Rationing, for godsake!
And there, beneath the balcony on which we stood,
the source of infinite energy. And all contained in one
small room designed for sport—a doubles court
for squash. And there the greatest gamesmanship
the world had ever seen. And you, Enrico, were
the referee. You with your slide rule and your
six-inch increments. December 2, 1942. The day
the moon lost all its shine, an absolute eclipse
you navigated, me at the helm, you screaming, "Hard
to port, Szilard! To port!" Two million Jews
in Europe dead, it was announced that day.
Five million more at risk. We hardly flinched.
We knew that day had made Jews of us all.

Ahimsa

Los Alamos
25 May 1943

Dear Fermi,
              Yes! Both Groves and Conant like your plan.
The radioactive isotopes bred in your pile and here
in these are numerous and certainly would do the trick.
Teller advises that the element that would surely have
the highest possibility is strontium because it would
get sent directly to the bones. And separating it,
he says, would be no problem. Still, for now it is
advisable that you delay until a safer future date
to help keep your plan quiet. We wouldn't, God forbid,
want German agents to get wind of it and beat us to
the punch. I somehow don't believe irradiated corn,
for instance, would appeal to an American's tongue!
Seriously, though, until we can be sure we're able to
kill at least a half a million men outright, delay
is best. I'm sure you understand. You are, after all,
like all of us, peace-loving—what, in Sanskrit, is
referred to as *ahimsa*: doing no harm or hurt.
You know, sometimes I wonder if this awful war
will ever end. We must do what we can.
                                    As Ever,
                                          Oppenheimer

A First Good Look

London
November 1943

Between September, when he began to think
seriously of escape, and early October,
when he completed it, the atom wasn't on his mind.
The Jews' fate was. Eight thousand of them,

Danish citizens all, massed like a nucleus
in Copenhagen. And the Nazis, threatening
to bombard them, mass back into nothing.
For a while our king and government managed

to forestall the inevitable. "You want our meat,
our bread and butter," they bartered. "We
want our Jews." And for a while the Nazis
stayed their steel and jackboots. Then

came August twenty-ninth and into Copenhagen
came their army. The future had arrived,
and it was grim. Exactly one month later
off my parents went, walking hand-in-hand

across the city. Until late that night,
like the most common criminals, they hid
among the filthy rakes and spades
in the gardening shed of a man who was

content with what his seeds brought forth,
flowers and foodstuffs fostered by his hand.
Imagine, in that rickety old shed the one
who'd plumbed the pure design of the seeds

of matter, of space and light; the one
who'd opened up the intricate design
of everything. A whole long day
evading death with the unknowing help

of a man whose only aim was coaxing life
from earth. What irony my father must
have felt, what dread as he awaited dark,
a scientist who'd committed decades

to stripping away layers of the dark;
a scientist who loved clear sight more
than the truth itself, more than himself,
more even than life. Without clear sight

there was no life. To see was everything,
and to reveal what he had seen—that
was the substance, the very reason, both
of his science and his life. In the atom,

he always said, there are no closed
societies, and what is good enough
for the atom is good enough for all
that is comprised of atoms—men,

and the things of men, especially.
God did, as he'd told Einstein, play
with dice, and they were strange dice,
too, themselves the *conditio sine qua non*

of all nature. God never lost, he said,
but the Nazis would, and they were not
good losers. That night my parents said
farewell to the gardener's shed and crossed

the Öresund in moonlight, missing patrols
and mines by little more than a breath,
and landed safe in Sweden—safe, that is,
for a few short days. My father met

the Swedish king, Gustaf, and told him
what he'd told Einstein: openness was
the proper thing. The times, he said,
demanded action. *Save the Danish Jews.*

And they did. Then he saved himself.
As did we all. But he went first, dressed
in an English flight suit and parachute
and carrying flares for the cold North Sea.

He took his place in the bomb bay
of a Mosquito, which would fly high
to avoid the German batteries, and was
outfitted with a helmet with earphones

and an oxygen mask. During all of this
the atom wasn't, as I've said, on his mind,
but by the time the Mosquito touched down
in Scotland it was. Perhaps the flight

had cleared his head, fainting the way
he had over Norway when he hadn't heard
the pilot say "attach your oxygen mask."
Perhaps in the thin Scandinavian air

visions had danced like atoms in his mind,
and seeds had taken root more blossom-bound
than those of the man who owned the shed.
The atom wasn't on his mind, but as they flew

low over the gray North Sea and set down
in Scotland, the visions came and he was set
to take a first good look. And what was it
he saw? Fear that the Germans had the key

to nature's armaments? Yes, that—and more.
Himself a bomb for that one desperate flight,
he saw the Bomb alone could rid the world
of bombs. Call it naïve, but by the time

his feet were rooted deep in English earth
he saw the world would henceforth have
to be a hothouse full of stems and roots.
It had no choice. And neither did he.

Beyond the Fields of Bright Aster

Los Alamos
December 1943

It was the most beautiful place
Segrè had seen. Botticelli would
have filled the fields of aster
with plump goddesses and nymphs
and set them dancing, wind
rippling hair the color of hay
and little angels hanging
in the air like drops
of early morning dew. Where
the jeep trail twisted through
the canyon that opened out
to a wooded valley in the midst
of which the cabin sat in a grove
of big-leaved trees, there were
markings cut in the steep walls,
the work of whole tribes of stone-
age artisans, etched equations
of the dazzling power of the nature
they danced for and prayed to,
invoking visions more seductive than
all our $E=MC^2$s. The Bomb,
it came to him, would be no more
than six feet long, its atoms,
as he imagined them, chain-
reacting to a glow beyond that
of all the fields of bright aster,
brilliances of a thousand gods,
their most collective roar the sun
imploding into harmonies more
voluptuous than the visions

depicted on the damp cave walls.
The gods had spoken. Atoms danced
in his head like savage men
around campfires. Little Boy was born.

The Journey of Death

"We thought of the legend of Prometheus...."

Los Alamos
July 1945

She phoned from Frisco, saying *come*.
He did, arriving on one warm evening
in mid-June. She met him in the station.

Then, according to our peeping-toms,
they left, stopping to admire the moon
three times, and went to her third-

floor apartment on Montgomery Street.
Believe, he said to her. But no,
she couldn't see, through such

enormous realms of dark, his god
and its promises of light. To her,
the new sun rose and the old went

down. And she was the old sun.
By twelve, our gumshoes tell us, they
retired. At eight he left. She stayed.

But she couldn't endure the dark,
the moon not enough. Nor his god.
And she wouldn't live half free.

In six short months she was gone,
the light put out by her own hand
on one cold January evening. *All*

I wanted, she said in her note,
was to give you all of me.
And so she went and he stayed,

convinced that in the desert his
god would come in a blinding flash
of light. Nothing could stop it now.

Soon it would come, turning sand
to jade, burning desert creatures
to charred lumps. He was sure of it.

Soon everyone would see heavens
churning, oceans of fire, the dawn
turning in an instant to high noon.

Nothing could stop it, this dragon-god,
this fire-breather, atom-mauler stirring
in its sleep. Ready to wake. To be.

And God help us, he was right.
One day we saw something in the sky
that lit the kindling of our minds.

It was only Venus, but even the frogs
began making love in every puddle,
ready to give themselves to it.

It was beautiful, and it set us free
to be the sons-of-bitches we'd have
to be to serve his god with the love

it would demand, to look it in the eye
and never flinch, to know the thing
we'd look upon to be a promise kept.

This god was real, and on that last
night, before it was born
in swaddling of such mass

the planet unraveled into fright
so powerful even men had to lie
in trenches like the dead and coat

their skin with lotions, he climbed
the tower for a last long look.
And the foul and awesome One was

the sun and the sun eclipsed. Was death.
Was life. It took his breath away.
But he'd done his duty. Now let him be.

When Chloroform No Longer Works

London
August 1964

Boredom was the worst. Day after day,
month after month, year after year—all four of them.
We'd all rather have faced off Jerry, even him,
the quietest suffering bloke there ever was.
We suffered, too, but not quietly, which might
have been one reason we didn't take to him right off.

It was fifty years ago this month, and though
I haven't laid eyes on him since the Armistice
I still can see him as he was the day the Krauts
shoved him through the gate so hard he landed face
down on the pile of piss-drenched hay that was our bed.

Dark and wirey-tough he was.
We used to joke amongst ourselves
about the beak that was his nose,
and we liked to say his forehead was
so bloody high it would be grand for cricket.

There were six of us,
all Englishmen caught in Berlin
at the start of the war,
and interred for the duration,
crammed in a stall built for two small horses.
So at first no one was too in love with anyone.

Through that first summer we sweltered.
One steamy day, when the smell of our own shit
was nearly making us heave, he laughed,
saying we really ought, like good scientists,
to separate our different elements by smell!
Bonkers, we thought, *he's bloody bonkers!*

Then we began to talk. And so did he,
of things we couldn't grasp, and some we did.

He said he felt like Gulliver and that,
for him, his ending up in Germany
had begun as a mistake. He'd meant,
at University, to read for Mathematics,
but found himself in the wrong place.

Physics, said the lecturer.

He said he liked the lecturer so he stayed.
Chasing invisible things became a way of life.
So did mistakes. Coming to Berlin was the first.
When war broke out his friends advised
he wait before attempting to sail home.
He did. That was his next mistake. He waited,
and then waited more. That was his third.

He was arrested, said to be a British spy.

He was, as someone said not long ago,
like one of his neutrons: invisible but there.
He talked, but never *really* said much,
in all those years complaining only once—
Nothing relative about loss, he snapped.

Since then, the only thing he's lost is sleep.
When chloroform no longer works,
nightmares advance, he told us once.
His was the Bomb. He didn't work on it,
but early on his work confirmed it could be done.
I'm sure that's why he started taking pills,
and hasn't missed since '41. Neither have we.

Notes

Wild Beasts...

"spectral lines...": Moseley determined the atomic number of every element up to zinc.

The poison gases actually smelled like new-mown hay and lilacs.

Clara's Calling

Electrons are the negatively-charged particles that "hop" from one "shell" (orbit) to another around the nucleus.

The Icehouse

An incident that really happened. Oppenheimer was fourteen, and his parents had sent him to a summer camp.

The Night that Nature...

Bohr and Erwin Schrödinger, another stunning physicist and philosopher, debated heatedly the nature of matter—whether it was particle (granular) or wave. The cat is an analogy for the complex relationship between the thing observed and the observer in the quantum realm.

The Dream of Doves

Szilard's prophetic vision of a chain reaction. The details of his escape from Germany are true.

The Birds of Passage...

Abraham Flexner established the Institute for Advanced Study at Princeton. He recruited Einstein.

All Things...

The drowning happened.

The Different Meanings...

Here Bohr is struggling with the problem of identity—another one of those dualities that "complementarity" helped to reconcile.

Wooden Tables...

"Urbino" was Michelangelo's faithful servant. The "Pope" alluded to is Julius II, for whom Michelangelo painted the Sistine Ceiling. The altar wall is an oblique reference to Michelangelo's *The Last Judgement*, painted more than two decades after the Sistine Ceiling, from 1534 to 1541. "Terribilità" was what Michelangelo's contemporaries called him. Trabacchi's status as a scholar of art is, as far as I know, fictional.

The Genius...

Bohr heard of Rutherford's death in Bologna, where he was attending a conference. The speech he gave, according to one of the participants, was the most moving he had ever heard.

Alpha particles are positively charged and consist of two protons and two neutrons.

The Day the Sand...

The "liquid-drop" was Bohr's conception of the atom. The nucleus was the "waist." Squeeze it and the nucleus splits in two, doubling itself. Fission occurs.

Back from the Vanishing...

Strauss was a source of finance for Szilard. Cablegrams, in those days, were the primary means of communication for scientists scattered all over Europe and America.

The Other I...

George Placzek was a theoretician. He challenged the relevance of Bohr's liquid-drop model of the nucleus. In the Peirels' analogy the window is the nucleus, the neutrons the balls. Bohr had one of his amazing insights, which he worked out on the blackboard in Einstein's office with three graphs. In short, he realized that U235, not U238, is the element that fissions in uranium. The question, fatally, was what would happen if you separated the two. We know now.

Queer Animals...

Rudolph Peirels and Otto Stern both went on to win a Nobel Prize in physics.

FDR & Me

Teller was at a conference. Franklin Roosevelt spoke. It seemed to Teller that Roosevelt was speaking directly to him. That was the turning point. The atom was his destiny.

Supping with...

The subject is Heisenberg's work for Nazi Germany. Bohr's rebuff must have been painful for both men.

The Day the Moon...

The occasion is the first atomic pile. The place is the University of Chicago. Fermi was the director of the project. Graphite bricks were used in the construction of the reactor.

Ahimsa

Leslie Groves, a general, and James B. Conant, president of Harvard and a distinguished chemist, were part of the council overseeing the Manhattan Project.

Strontium is a deadly radioactive isotope that Fermi thought could be used to irradiate the German food supply. The body takes it in in place of calcium. It works its way into the bones.

A First Good Look

Aage Bohr is the speaker. The events of Bohr's escape are accurate. He did, in fact, convince the Swedish government to offer sanctuary to Denmark's Jewish citizens. All but a small number escaped.

"...there are no closed societies" means just that. At worst, that is, the atom is a constitutional monarchy, not a dictatorship. If the nuclei are kings, the electrons are the parliaments. Bohr argued that the same would have to be true of the world. Another application of his "complementarity."

Beyond the Fields…

The size of the Bomb was a problem from the start. Segrè solved the problem.

The Journey of Death

Jean Tatlock was Oppenheimer's early love and former fiancée whom he visited in San Francisco in June of 1943, under surveillance as always. She actually did commit suicide in January of 1944.

The first atomic explosion, code-named *Trinity* by Oppenheimer, occurred on July 16, 1945 in an area about 200 miles south of Los Alamos—in Spanish the *Jornada del Muerto*: the Journey of Death.

When Chloroform…

Although the speaker is fictional, Chadwick did in fact spend the war years as a prisoner of war in Germany.

George Drew

George Drew was born in Mississippi and raised there and in New York State, where he currently resides. *Toads in a Poisoned Tank*, his first book, was published in 1986, and a chapbook, *So Many Bones (Poems of Russia)*, in 1997 by a Russian press, in a bilingual edition. One of his poems received an Honorable Mention in the Robert Frost Foundation's poetry competition, 2002, and another in the W.B. Yeats Society's competition, the same year. He was awarded a residency at the Vermont Studio Center in 2004, and that summer he was a Guest Poet at The Frost Place in Franconia, NH. He was the winner of the 2003 Paumanok Poetry Award.

CPSIA information can be obtained at www.ICGtesting.com
Printed in the USA
BVOW03s0845190314

348030BV00002B/26/P